Learn French In 7 DAYS!

The Ultimate Crash Course to Learning the Basics of the French Language in No Time

By Dagny Taggart

Disclaimer

The information provided in this book is designed to provide helpful information on the subjects discussed. The author's books are only meant to provide the reader with the basics knowledge of a certain language, without any warranties regarding wheter the student will, or will not, be able to incorporate and apply all the information provided. Although the writer will make her best effort share her insights, language learning is a difficult task, and each person needs a different timeframe to fully incorporate a new language. This book, nor any of the author's books constitute a promise that the reader will learn a certain language within a certain timeframe.

Table of Contents

"La description physique" (physical aspect)
"AIMER" (to like)
"Test your French!"

Chapter 4 : The French "Gourmet" Culture

Gastronomy & fine food
All about meals
Dining out
How to order food and drinks?
A drink at the bar
"Test your French!"

Chapter 5 : Travelling Around

Locating yourself
Transportation
Fun in town
Facing emergencies
"Test your French!"

Chapter 6 : Business Matters

The workplace
Doing business
Planning a business trip
"Test your French!"

Chapter 7 : All About Numbers

Let's count
Ordinal numbers ("les nombres ordinaux")
Cardinal numbers ("les nombres cardinaux")
The clock is ticking
How much money?
"Test your French!"

Conclusion: Now, Embark on Your Own Adventure!

Preview Of "Learn Spanish In 7 DAYS! - The Ultimate Crash Course To Learn The Basics of the Spanish Language In No Time"

Dedicated to those who love going beyond their own frontiers.

Keep on traveling,

Dagny Taggart

Introduction

Why should YOU learn French?

Backpacking in the South of France? Dating a dreamy French man or a beautiful French lady? Planning a business meeting with French clients? Moving to a French-speaking country? Willing to show off at the next French festival of your local town?...

This book is for ALL OF YOU!

Thanks to this book, you'll get a grasp of what is French and how to master it! This book will offer you a complete overview of the language along with useful expressions to start speaking.

French is a difficult language to learn... that's why this book makes it fun and easy... without forgetting efficiency!

By the end of this course, you will get the amazing feeling that YOU CAN DO IT! YOU CAN SPEAK FRENCH!

How will YOU learn French within a few weeks?

Are you aware that as an English speaker, you already know some 15,000 French words. The English language has indeed been shaped by many other languages, such as Latin, German, French.

The French influence on English dates back to the Norman invasion of England in 1066. It had a major impact not only on the country but on the language itself. William the Conqueror brought Norman French which became the language of the court, the government and the upper class for the next three centuries. During the Norman occupation, around 10,000 French words were adopted into English, of which about 75% are still used today. More than 30% of all English words are derived directly or indirectly from French.

If that doesn't convince you to learn French, the idea of visiting one of the 33 French-speaking countries over the world might do it!

French and English are the only languages spoken as a native language on 5 continents and the only languages taught in every country in the world. French is the official or one of the official languages in 33 countries[1]. This number is second to English, which is officially spoken in 45 countries.

Let's not wait anymore and indulge yourself in our learning program... and most of all, ENJOY every bit of the journey!

---

1   French is the official language of France and its overseas territories (French Guyana, Guadeloupe, Martinique, Mayotte, La Réunion, French Polynesia, New Caledonia, Saint Barts, Saint Martin, Saint Pierre and Miquelon, Wallis and Futuna) as well as 14 other countries: Bénin, Burkina Faso, Central African Republic, Democratic Republic of Congo, Republic of Congo, Côte d'Ivoire, Gabon, Guinea, Luxembourg, Mali, Monaco, Niger, Sénégal, Togo.

French is also one of the official languages in the following countries: Belgium, Burundi, Cameroon, Canada, Chad, Channel Islands (Guernsey and Jersey), Comoros, Djibouti, Equatorial, Guinea, Haiti (the other official language is French Creole), Madagascar, Rwanda, Seychelles, Switzerland, Vanuatu.

Chapter 1: Introducing French

What you're about to learn:

➜ How to use French words you already know
➜ How to be at ease with French pronounciation

French/English similarities

The Normans brought French into the English language which resulted in more than 30% of French words currently being used by English natives. You may not be aware of it but everyday... you speak French!

Many of the words of French origin used in English find their roots in Latin and/or Greek. As an example, "beef" from French "boeuf" is meat from a cow (from old English "cu") which is a type of "bovine" from Latin "bovinus" via French "bovin".

For a clearer comprehension of the similarities, we have divided this paragraph into four different aspects related to the French influence in English language. There are original French words and expressions to be found in English, true cognates ("vrais amis"), false cognates ("faux amis") and spelling equivalents.

This will make it easier to understand how to use French words you already know and use in English!

French words & expressions in English

Over the years, an important number of French words and expressions have been absorbed by the English language and are still intact. Many English speakers might not even realize that they are using these French words in everyday conversations.
Some other words and expressions have been kept to add *a certain touch of French* – "un certain je ne sais quoi". English speakers seem to be aware of this French influence and intentionally using those words with a somewhat accurate pronunciation!

Below is a list of some common examples of French words and expressions used in English.

"adieu" : farewell

"à la carte" : on the menu

"à la mode" : in fashion/style (in English "with ice-cream")

"art déco" : decorative art

"au pair" : a person who works for a family in exchange for room and board

"avant-garde" : innovative (arts)

"brunette" : small, dark-haired female

"cordon bleu" : master chef

"coup d'état" : government overthrow

"cuisine" : type of food/cooking

"débutante" : beginner (In French, "débutante" is the feminine form of "débutant" which means in English beginner (noun) or beginning (adj). In both languages, it refers to a young girl making her formal début into society. Interestingly this usage is not original in French. It was adopted back from English.)

"déjà-vu" : feeling like you've already seen or done something

"haute couture" : high-class clothing style

"Mardi Gras" : Shrove Tuesday

"pot-pourri" : cented mixture of dried flowers and spices

"prêt-à-porter" : clothing

"savoir-faire" : know-how

"savoir-vivre" : manners, etiquette

"souvenir" : memento

"Bon appétit!" : Enjoy your meal!

"Bon voyage!" : Have a good trip!

"C'est la vie!" : That's life!

"Oh là là!" : Ooh la la!

"RSVP" ("Répondez s'il vous plaît") : Please RSVP

"Touché!" : You got me!

"Voilà!" : There it is!

True cognates ("vrais amis")

True cognates (true friends) are words with identical spelling and meaning in both French and English. Given the great use of these words in English, you already have a considerable asset to start using French vocabulary!

True cognates are pronounced differently most of the time. However the exact spelling makes it a great advantage to learn French as an English speaker. You can easily learn some French phrases that have several true cognates.

For instance, "je vais voir un film au cinéma ce week-end avec mon cousin" can be understood with the words "film", "cinema", "weekend" and "cousin". You can easily come up with a translation thanks to the French cognates: "I will go to the movies this weekend with my cousin".

Note: "cousin" is used in both French and English to refer to the son (or daughter in English) of one of your sibling. While it remains the same for male and female in English, the feminine form has a different spelling in French: "cousin<u>e</u>".

Did you really think that it was so hard to speak French? Just start using the hundreds of words you already use everyday!
The list of French cognates is incredibly long – they are estimated to be some 1,700 words! The following list is just a sample of some of the most common true cognates used in English.

Useful to learn French:

"accent" (masculine noun)
"alphabet" (masculine)

Useful words at work:

"absence" (feminine noun)
"accident" (masculine)
"client" (masculine)
"collaboration" (feminine)
"communication" (feminine)
"contact" (masculine)
"document" (masculine)
"fax" (masculine)
"message" (masculine)
"mission" (feminine)

"obligation" (feminine)
"payable" (adjective)
"profession" (feminine)
"solution" (feminine)
"test" (masculine)

Planning your weekend get-away:

"barbecue" (masculine)
"bikini" (masculine)
"bistro" (masculine)
"bungalow" (masculine)
"camp" (masculine)
"casino" (masculine)
"concert" (masculine)
"kayak" (masculine noun)
"parachute" (masculine)
"parasol" (masculine)
"promenade" (feminine)
"ski" (masculine)
"sport" (masculine)
"taxi" (masculine)
"tennis" (masculine)
"valise" (feminine)
"zoo" (masculine)

At the restaurant:

"addition" (feminine)
"apéritif" (masculine)
"chef" (masculine)
"dessert" (masculine)
"entrée" (feminine)
"fruit" (masculine)
"gourmet" (masculine)
"hors-d'oeuvre" (masculine)
"menu" (masculine)
"pizza" (feminine)
"quiche" (feminine)
"sorbet" (masculine)
"steak" (masculine)
"vodka" (feminine)

False cognates ("faux-amis")

In French, there are numerous "faux-amis" (false cognates or false friends). These words can cause communication problems as they look alike in French and English but have a totally different meaning.

A wrong use of a false friend can end up by a funny joke or a lack of respect. As an example, it can be funny to hear that someone never buys food containing "préservatifs", which in French means "condoms"! However it would not be clever to mistake "pain", which means "bread" in French, with the actual English word (the correct French word being "douleur"). You never know what you will end up getting at the drugstore!

Here is a list of the most common "faux-amis" to avoid stupid mistakes that will haunt you forever!

French faux ami	English translation
actuel	Current, present
actuellement	Currently, presently
agenda	diary
allure	pace, appearance, style
assister à	to attend
attendre	to wait
avertissement	warning
balance	scale
blesser	to wound
bribes	fragments
car	coach
cave	cellar
chair	flesh
chance	luck
coin	corner
déception	disappointment
demander	to ask for
éventuellement	possibly
fabrique	factory
formidable	terrific
génial	brilliant

gentil	kind
injures	insult
lecture	reading
nouvelle	piece of news, short story
patron	boss
préservatif	condom
procès	trial
prune	plum
quitter	to leave
rester	to stay
sensible	sensitive
tissu	fabric

The use of "Franglais"

"Franglais" refers to the massive invasion of French by English words and expressions thanks to the globalization, bringing a worldwide popular culture, and the access to the internet. It has become trendy to use English words in French language. Despite many efforts, the French have failed into translating these English words in their own language, unlike the Canadian French who remarkably succeed in finding equivalents for every English word!

Below is a short list of the most common English words used by French speakers:

baby-foot	table football
basket	Sports shoe, basketball
brushing	blow-dry
camping	campsite
dressing	walk-in closet
catch	wrestling
flipper	pinball machine
footing	jogging
forcing	pressure
jogging	tracksuit
lifting	face-lift
people	celebrity
planning	schedule
pressing	dry-cleaner

relooking	make-over
smoking	tuxedo
sweat	sweatshirt
warning	hazard lights

Pronunciation

The French alphabet has the same number of letters as the English one. There are 6 vowels ("une voyelle") and 20 consonants ("une consonne").

A **vowel** is a sound that is pronounced through the mouth (or the nose for nasal vowels) with no obstruction of the lips, tongue, or throat.
There are a few general guidelines to keep in mind when pronouncing French vowels:
➔Most French vowels are pronounced further forward in the mouth than their English counterparts.
➔The tongue must remain tensed throughout the pronunciation of the vowel.

As for the **consonants**, many of them are similar in French and English so they should be quite easy to learn.

As an approach to French pronunciation ("la prononciation"), we propose you to use the following guide throughout the chapters.

Always refer to this pronunciation guide whenever you try to say a French word from our book. You can also complement your studies with vocal guides to be easily found on the Internet.

Simple letters ("les lettres simples"):

French letters	Sounds like	English examples	French examples
a	a	r[a]t	bras (arm), chat (cat)
b	b	[b]utter	bateau (boat), bébé (baby)
c before o,a,u	k	[c]andy	carte (map), col (collar)
c before e,i,y	s	[s]tanza	citron (lemon), ciment (cement)
ç	s	[s]ilence	ça (this), garçon (boy)
d	d	[d]og	dos (back), dans (in)

e	u	b[u]bble	le (the), ce (this)
f	f	[f]ood	faire (to make), fleur (flower)
g before o,a,u	g	[g]row	gauche (left), guerre (war)
g before e,i,y	j	dé[j]à vu	orange (orange), girafe (giraffe)
h always silent	_	_	hibou (owl), hache (ax)
i	ee	f[ee]t	bisou (kiss), cri (shout)
j	j	dé[j]à vu	je (I), jamais (never)
k	k	[k]oala	képi (kepi), koala (koala)
l	l	[l]ove	lapin (rabbit), livre (book)
m	m	[m]other	maman (mom), mon (mine)
n	n	[n]ever	non (no), nid (nest)
o	o	z[o]rro	domino (domino), collègue (colleague)
p	p	[p]asta	papa (dad), patate (potatoe)
q	q	[c]ap	quatre (four), qui (who)
r	r	a[r]t deco	rare (unsual), radis (radish)
s	s	[s]nail	son (sound), savoir (know)
t	t	[t]ag	tata (auntie), ton (your)
u	ew	déjà v[u]	tu (you), ruban (ribbon)
v	v	[v]iew	vivre (to live), venir (to come)
w	v	wa[v]e	wagon
w (English origin)	w	[w]ater	whisky, wapiti
x inside a word or when ex- is followed by a consonnant or at the end of words	x	e[x]cess	expert, luxe (luxury)

x at the begining of a word or when ex- is followed by a vowel or h	x	e[x]am	exemple (example), examen (exam, test)
x at the end of words	s	[s]olution	dix (ten), six (six)
x (rare cases)	z	[z]ero	deuxième (second)
x at the end of words to indicate plural	silent	–	choux (cabbages), chevaux (horses)
y	y	[y]am	yoyo, yacht
z	z	[z]ip	zéro (zero), zèbre (zebra)

Complex sounds ("les sons complexes"):

French sounds	Sounds like	English examples	French examples
ai	ai	l[ai]ssez-faire	aimer (to love), faire (to do)
-ain, -aim	un	Verd[un]	pain (bread), faim (hunger)
au	o	r[o]pe	paume (palm), baume (balm)
ch	sh	[sh]ampoo	château (castle), chapeau (hat)
ei	e	m[e]n	peine (pain), reine (queen)
eu	e	th[e]	peu (little), deux (two)
-er, -ez	a	d[a]y	manger (to eat), vous allez (you go)
eau, -aud, -ot	o	[o]zone	rateau (rake), chaud (hot), pot (jar)
em, en before consonant	en	[en]core	entre (between), emploi (job)
ha-	a	r[a]t	habiter (to live)

ill	y	[y]ogurt	fille (girl), billet (ticket)
oi	wa	[wa]ter	toit (roof), quoi (what)
oin	oo + un	t[oo]+Verd[un]	loin (far), coin (corner)
on, om	on	s[on]g	bon (good), chanson (song)
ou	oo	t[wo]	fou (crazy), cou (neck)
ph	f	[f]ather	phare (lighthouse)
sc before o,a,u	sc	[sc]oundrel	sculpter (to sculpt), scorpion
sc before e,i,y	sc	[sc]enario	scie (saw), scène (stage)
th	t	[t]ime	thym (thyme), thèse (thesis)
ti	s	[s]tone	objection (objection), prophétie (prophecy)
um, un word ending or before a consonant	un	Verd[un]	un (a), parfum (perfume)
ui	wi	ki[wi]	pluie (rain), cuisine (kitchen)

Accents ("les accents")

French letters	Sounds like	English examples	French examples
à	a	r[a]t	à (in)
é	a	d[a]y	école (school), café (coffee)
è, ê	e	m[e]n	père (father), mère (mother)
â,î,ô,û pronounced as a,i,o,u			château (castle), hôpital (hospital) ...
ä, ë, ï, ö, ü the tréma indicates that the two adjacent	a i	n[a i]ve	Noël (Christmas), haïr (to hate)

vowels	must
both	be
pronounced	

Let's review what you've learnt in that chapter with a few exercises.

Mark the correct answers:

In French, "people" is used to mean:
□ a young person
□ an old person
□ a celebrity

In English, "brilliant" is the translation of the following French word:
□ brilliant
□ épatant
□ génial

In French, "brunette" refers to :
□ a type of food
□ a small, dark-haired female
□ a painting color

Which of the following words is a true cognate (true friend)?"
□ actually
□ car
□ pot-pourri

Which of the following is a false cognate (false friend)?
□ préservatif
□ débutante
□ gourmet

Which of the following English term uses the French sound "eau" like in "chapeau" (hat)?
□ face
□ throw
□ shampoo

Which of the following English term uses the French sound "ai" like in "aimer" (to love)?

□ well
□ parade
□ three

Answers:

In French, "people" is used to mean:
□ a celebrity

In English, "brilliant" is the translation of the following French word:
□ génial

In French, "brunette" refers to :
□ a small, dark-haired female

Which of the following words is a true cognate (true friend)?"
□ pot-pourri

Which of the following is a false cognate (false friend)?
□ préservatif

Which of the following English term uses the French sound "eau" like in "chapeau" (hat)?
□ throw

Which of the following English term uses the French sound "ai" like in "aimer" (to love)?
□ well

Chapter 2 : Grammar Basics

What you're about to learn:

➜ How to make simple sentences in French
➜ How to ask questions of which you can easily understand the answer
➜ How to understand the most common grammar rules and usage

The sentence

How to make a sentence? This is an useful thing to learn, isn't it?

The structure of a sentence in French is not too different from the English. However there are exceptions to every rule in French grammar which makes it a bit tricky. But don't run away yet! By the end of this chapter, you will be able to make simple sentences without having to worry too much about the rules.

The most simple way of forming a sentence is as follows:

Noun [N] or Pronoun [P]+Verb [V] + Adjective [Adj] or Adverb [Adv]

"La fille [N] est [V] jolie [Adj]" = the girl is pretty
or
"Le garçon [N] parle [V] fort [Adv]" = the boy speaks loudly
or
"Elle [P] marche [V] lentement [Adv]" = she walks slowly

In order to form this type of sentence, you need to understand how to use each one of the combined terms : the noun, the pronoun, the verb, the adjective and the adverb.

The noun ("le nom")

You have to follow a few important rules to properly use a noun in French.

First : Every noun has a gender, masculine or feminine, unlike English neutral nouns.

Second : Every noun has an article preceeding the noun.

Third : Every noun can be either singular or plural – it is called the number.

You need to keep in mind that there is hardly any way of guessing if a noun is feminine or masculine. When you learn a new noun, try to learn its article at the same time.

Singular masculine articles are "le" (the) and "un" (a).

Singular feminine articles are "la" (the), "une" (a).

Plural masculine or feminine articles are "les" (the), "des" (some).

The articles "le", "la", "les" are known as "articles définis" (definite articles).
The articles "un", "une", "des" are known as "articles indéfinis" (indefinite articles).

For example, you will learn how to say "table", which is the exact same word in French with a different pronunciation though.

"la table" = the table = feminine definite article

"une table" = a table = feminine indefinite article

Below is a shortlist of a few nouns and their definite and indefinite articles:

English	Definite singular	Indefinite singular	Definite plural	Indefinite plural
house	la maison	une maison	les maisons	des maisons
bag	le sac	un sac	les sacs	des sacs
car	la voiture	une voiture	les voitures	des voitures
bicycle	le vélo	un vélo	les vélos	des vélos

Note: For plural nouns, you have to add an extra "s" at the end of the noun. This is the common mark for the plural form.

Your turn to practise! Fill up the following table:

bus	le bus	… bus	… bus
bedroom	… …	une chambre	... chambres
book	… livre	… …	… livres
kitchen	… …	une cuisine	… …

The pronoun ("le pronom")

Pronouns can replace nouns in a sentence. There are different types of pronouns in French, which can be divided into two main categories: personal pronouns ("pronoms personnels") and impersonal pronouns ("pronoms impersonnels").

The personal pronouns refer to the person who is speaking or the subject of the sentence. The impersonal pronouns do not refer to a person or a specific subject. In the sentence "il neige" (it is snowing), "il" is an impersonal pronoun as it doesn't refer to anyone or anything in particular. The impersonal pronouns are mostly use with impersonal verbs, such as "neiger" (to snow).

Let's focus now on the easiest pronouns. For a clearer understanding, you will find below a table summarizing the most common pronouns. Notice that English pronouns have their equivalents in French. Easy, right ?!!

je	I	mon/ma	my	moi	me
tu	you	ton/ta	your	toi	you
il/elle	he/she	son/sa	his/her	lui/elle	he/she
nous	we	notre	our	nous	us
vous	you	votre	your	vous	you
ils/elles	they	leurs	their	eux	them

Let's look at a few examples:

"**Je** parle anglais."
I speak English.

"**Ma** mère parle français."
My mother speaks French.

"Julie, c'est **moi**!"
Julie, it's me!

"C'est **mon** livre."
That's my book.

The verb ("le verbe")

A verb tells you what is the action or the state of the noun being the subject of the action or state.

The subject can be a noun ("la table") or a pronoun ("tu").
The common rule is the same as in English : you need to conjugate the verb according to the noun or the pronoun used.

Example:
"La fille est jolie." = The girl is pretty.
> "la fille" is a singular feminine noun; the verb is conjugated in singular: "est".

"Les filles sont jolies." = The girls are pretty.
> "les filles" is a plural feminine noun; the verb is conjugated in plural: "sont".

Let's just learn right now a few verbs which are very similar in French and English.
Note: the verbs are written in their infinitive form ("l'infinitif").

"danser" = to dance
"désirer" = to desire
"camper" = to camp
"former" = to form
"modifier" = to modify
"photographier" = to photograph
"regretter" = to regret
"signer" = to sign
"tester" = to test

The adjective ("l'adjectif")

The purpose of an adjective is to describe a noun. As gender and number rules apply, the adjective has to match the gender and the number of the noun it is associated with.

Examples:
"le petit appartement" = the small apartment
"appartement" is a singular masculine noun, its pronoun is singular masculine : "le".

"la jupe bleue" = the blue skirt
"jupe" is a singular feminine noun, its pronoun is singular feminine : "la"

"des enfants sages" = the well-behaved kids
"enfants" is a plural masculine noun, its pronoun is plural : "des"

As you may have noticed, French people just love being unpredictable. Keep in mind that adjectives can be placed before or after the nouns!

There is a useful rule related to the position of the adjective. Adjectives preceding a noun usually refer to **beauty, age, goodness or badness, size**.

Examples:
"une jolie femme" = a pretty woman
"un jeune garçon" = a young boy
"une bonne glace" = a good ice-cream
"une grande maison" = a big house

The adverb ("l'adverbe")

The adverb can be used instead of the adjective in the simple sentence form: "N + V + Adv".
It describes the verb it refers to. In English, most adverbs end with "-ly" while in French they end with "-ment".

Examples:
"Les oiseaux chantent **gaiement**." = The birds sing happily.
"Ma grand-mère parle **doucement**." = My grand-mother speaks softly/slowly.
"Je marche très **rapidement**." = I walk very fast.

Questions & Answers

Asking questions in French is actually much easier than in English.
The easiest and most popular way is by <u>just raising the voice at the end of the sentence</u>. The person you are talking to will understand that you are not making a statement but asking a question.

Examples:
"Tu as faim?" = Are you hungry?
"Vous avez un plan?" = Do you have a map?

If you wish to adopt a more formal tone, you need <u>to invert subject and verb</u> as follows :

Tu as faim? => **As-tu** faim?
Vous avez un plan? => **Avez-vous** un plan?

The above questions will be answered by yes or no.
To form a question requiring a specific piece of information (who, where, when...), you need to use a question word.

Below are the most common question words used in French:

"quand" = when
"qui" = who
"quoi" = what
"où" = where
"pourquoi" = why
"combien" = how many/much

Examples:

"Tu pars quand?" = When are you leaving?
"Qui est le patron?" = Who is the boss?
"Tu fais quoi? = What are you doing?
"Elle travaille où?" = Where does she work?
"Pourquoi pleures-tu?" = Why are you crying?
"Combien coûte le chapeau?" = How much costs the hat?

To answer the question, you can either answer with a positive statement ("une affirmation") or a negative statement ("une négation").
The "affirmation" usually starts with "oui" (yes), whereas the "négation" usually starts with "non" (no).

Look at the following examples:

"Vous avez un plan? **Oui, nous avons** un plan!"
Do you have a map? Yes, we do!

"Tu as faim? **Non, je n'ai pas** faim."
Are you hungry? No, I'm not.

"Tu vas à New York demain? **Oui, je vais** à New York demain."
Are you going to New York tomorrow? Yes, I am."

"Tu vas à Paris demain? **Non, je ne vais pas** à Paris demain."
Are you going to Paris tomorrow? No, I'm not."

"ne (+verbe) pas" is the typical form to make a negative sentence. The verb located in between "ne" and "pas" is conjugated. When the verb starts with a vowel, "ne" becomes "**n'**".

Let's take a few more examples to be sure that you got it right!

"Je **ne** suis **pas** malade."

I'm not sick.

"Il **ne** dort **pas** beaucoup."
He doesn't sleep much.

"Nous **n'**avons **pas** de veste."
We don't have any jacket.

Simple tenses

Same as in English, there are two types of verbs : *regular* ("régulier") and *irregular* ("irrégulier"). This will have an influence on their conjugation. But remember that the best way to conjugate a verb in French is not by guessing but by <u>learning each type of irregular forms</u>!

Let's be real. You will not learn every type of conjugation here. However our objective is to help understand the different patterns.

Regular or irregular? ("Régulier ou irrégulier?")

In both English and French, there are two different types of conjugation for a verb: regular or irregular.
Regular verbs are the ones following the common conjugation rules. In simple words, they are easy to conjugate by adding a simple ending to their infinitive form.

Regular verbs are divided into 3 main groups:

➜ first group : endings in **"-ER"**
Ex.: "parler" (to talk), "manger" (to eat), "travailler" (to work)

➜ second group : endings in **"-IR"**
Ex.: "finir" (to finish), "choisir" (to choose), "grandir" (to grow up)

➜ third group : endings in **"-RE"**
Ex.: "attendre" (to wait), "entendre" (to hear), "vendre" (to sell)

Note: Be careful! <u>Some verbs with the endings -ER, -IR and -RE are irregular</u>!

Irregular verbs are the ones following a different conjugation. There is no rule, you need to memorize their conjugation by heart!

Here are the most common irregular verbs:

"être" = to be
"avoir" = to have
"pouvoir" = to be able to
"vouloir" = to want
"devoir" = to need to
"aller" = to go
"venir" = to come
"apprendre" = to learn
"comprendre" = to understand
"faire" = to do
"dire" = to say
"voir" = to see
"savoir" = to know
"croire" = to believe

Present tense ("le présent")

Same as in English, if you want to talk about something happening right now, you will use the simple present tense ("le présent de l'indicatif").
The conjugation for regular verbs is rather easy in present tense.

Let's take a look at a few examples from each group of the regular type and note the ending of the verbs.

parler	je parle	I talk
	tu parles	you talk
	il/elle parle	he/she talks
	nous parlons	we talk
	vous parlez	you talk
	ils/elles parlent	they talk
choisir	je choisis	I choose
	tu choisis	you choose
	il/elle choisit	he/she chooses
	nous choisissons	we choose
	vous choisissez	you choose
	ils/elles choisissent	they choose

attendre	j'atten**ds**	I wait
	tu atten**ds**	you wait
	il/elle atten**d**	he/she waits
	nous atten**dons**	we wait
	vous atten**dez**	you wait
	ils/elles atten**dent**	they wait

Past tense ("le passé")

One of the easiest and most common way to express past actions is the past perfect tense ("le passé composé"). It is composed of an auxiliary verb "être" (to be) or "avoir" (to have) and the past participle of the action verb. The auxiliary verb is conjugated in present tense.

être (to be)	avoir (to have)
je **suis**	j'**ai**
tu **es**	tu **as**
il/elle **est**	il/elle **a**
nous **sommes**	nous **avons**
vous **êtes**	vous **avez**
ils **sont**	ils **ont**

Examples:

"j'ai parlé" = I spoke
"tu as chanté" = you sang
"elle est partie" = she left

Below are a few examples of regular verbs conjugated in past tense:

j'ai parlé	I talked	j'ai choisi	I chose
tu **as parlé**	you talked	tu **as choisi**	you chose
il/elle **a parlé**	he/she talked	il/elle **a choisi**	he/she chose
nous **avons parlé**	we talked	nous **avons choisi**	we chose
vous **avez parlé**	you talked	vous **avez choisi**	you chose

ils/elles **ont parlé**	they talked	ils/elles **ont choisi**	they chose

Future tense ("le futur")

Whenever you want to refer to a future action, you have two options:

- the similar expression as in English "to be going to" (in French "aller faire")

Ex.: "Elle **va travailler**." = She is going to work.

Here is the conjugation of the irregular verb "aller" (to go):

Je **vais**	I go
Tu **vas**	you go
Il/elle **va**	he/she go
Nous **allons**	we go
Vous **allez**	you go
Ils/elles **vont**	they go

- the future tense

Ex.: "Elle apprendra le français l'année prochaine." = She will learn French next year.

The future tense is rather simple in its conjugation. You need to add the following endings to the infinitive form of the verb:
-ai, -as, -a, -ons, -ez, -ont

Note: Whenever the infinitive form ends with a vowel such as "attendre", you will simply get rid of the last "e" to add the endings of the future tense.

Below are examples of regular verbs conjugated in future tense:

j'attend**rai**	I will wait	je manger**ai**	I will eat
Tu attendr**as**	you will wait	tu manger**as**	you will eat
Il/elle attendr**a**	he/she will wait	il/elle manger**a**	he/she will eat
Nous attendr**ons**	we will wait	nous manger**ons**	we will eat
Vous attendr**ez**	you will wait	vous manger**ez**	you will eat

| Ils/elles attend**ront** | they will wait | ils/elles mange**ront** | they will eat |

"Le vouvoiement"

"Le vouvoiement" refers to the formal way of addressing someone in French.

In French, it is indeed important to be careful on the way you address a person. There is a special mark of politeness that you shouldn't skip or else you will sound really rude!

When you address someone you don't know or hardly know, you should use the pronoun "vous" as a more polite and respectful form of the English "you". You will conjugate it the same way you do for the plural form of "you". This formal pronoun can be used for both one person or several ones.

Ex.: "Comment allez-vous?" = How are you?

Whenever you are talking to an elder person or a person at work from a higher rank, the same rule applies.

Our recommendation: To avoid any etiquette mistake, we highly advise you not to use the pronoun "tu" unless the other person is using it.

"Test your French!"

Let's review what you've learnt in that chapter with a few exercises.

<u>Mark the correct answers:</u>

"Tu as faim?"
□ Oui, je n'ai pas faim.
□ Non, je n'ai pas faim.
□ Non, elle n'a pas faim.

"Quand allez-vous à Paris?"
□ Je vais à New York.
□ Nous allons à Paris demain.
□ Tu ne vas pas à Paris.

"Sa mère parle français?"
□ Oui, son père parle français.

□ Non, sa mère ne parle pas anglais.
□ Oui, sa mère parle français.

Fill the gaps:

Il a … jolie voiture.
… oiseaux chantent gaiement.
C'est ... petit appartement!
… jupe est bleue.
Tu as … enfants très sages.

Translate the sentence:

I speak French and English. = …
She eats a good ice-cream. = …
Are you waiting for the boss? = …
We chose a blue jacket. = …
I don't sleep much. = …
Are you sick? No, I'm not. = …

Answers:

□ Non, je n'ai pas faim.
□ Nous allons à Paris demain.
□ Oui, sa mère parle français.

Il a une jolie voiture.
Les oiseaux chantent gaiement.
C'est un/mon/son petit appartement.
La/sa/ma jupe est bleue.
Tu as des enfants très sages.

Je parle français et anglais.
Elle mange une bonne glace.
Vous attendez le patron? OR Attendez-vous le patron?
Nous avons choisi une veste bleue.
Je ne dors pas beaucoup.
Tu es malade? Non, je ne suis pas malade.

Chapter 3 : Greetings & Small Talk

What you're about to learn:

- → How to greet people with proper manners
- → How to speak about yourself and the others
- → How to enjoy small talk and make new friends

Congrats! You successfully passed the most difficult part! Grammar and pronunciation are complicated in French but once you know the basics, you can learn anything with greater skills. Let's start talking and not wasting any time to prepare you for your trip to Paris!

Greetings

Let's say hi!

in the morning : "bonjour!"
in the evening : "bonsoir!"
at night : "bonne nuit!"
informal : "salut!"
have a good day! : "bonne journée!"

Let's see each other later!

"aurevoir!" : good bye!
"à bientôt!" : see you soon!
"à plus tard!" : see you later!
"à plus!" : later!
"à demain!" : see you tomorrow!
"salut!" : bye! (informal)

How are you? I'm fine!

"La question" (question)
informal : "Ça va?"
standard : "Comment ça va?" or "Comment vas-tu?" or "Tu vas bien?"
formal : "Comment allez-vous?"

"La réponse affirmative" (positive answer)
informal : "Ça va!"
standard : "Ça va (très) bien!"

formal : "Je vais (très) bien, merci !"

"La réponse affirmative" (negative answer)
informal : "Ça va pas."
standard : "Non, ça ne va pas bien."
formal : "Non, je ne vais pas bien.

Note:
"bien" means good, "très bien" means very good.
"affirmation" (affirmative form) = "Oui!"
"négation" (negative form) = "Non!"

"Petite conversation avec un ami" (small talk with a friend) :

"Salut! Tu vas bien?"
"Ça va!" or "Je vais très bien!"
"Et toi, ça va?"
"Ça va bien! A bientôt!"
"Bonne journée!"

"Quelques formules de politesse" (polite manners):
"S'il vous plaît!" : please!
"Merci!" : thank you!
"Excusez-moi!" : Excuse-me!
"Désolé!" : sorry!
"Pardon!" : pardon-me!

Below are a few expressions useful to remember.

"Excusez-moi, je ne comprends pas."
Excuse-me, I don't understand.

"Pouvez-vous répéter, s'il vous plaît?"
Can you repeat, please?

"Merci, j'ai compris!"
Thank you, I understood!

"Je suis désolé, ce n'est pas facile de parler français!"
I'm sorry, it's not easy to speak French!

"Pardon, que dis-tu?"
Pardon-me, what are you saying?

"S'il vous plaît, comment on prononce ce mot?"
Please, how do you pronounce that word?

"Je m'excuse mais c'est faux!"
My apologies but it is not correct!

"Oui, je suis d'accord avec vous!"
Yes, I agree with you!

Introducing yourself

"LE NOM" (name)

"le prénom" : first name
"le nom de famille" : last name

To say your name, there is only one verb : "s'appeler". This verb is a special one; it is a reflexive verb ("un verbe pronominal"). Be careful of how you conjugate it!

"Je **m'**appelle" = my name is
"Tu **t'**appelles" = your name is
"Il/elle **s'**appelle" = his/her name is
"Nous **nous** appelons" = our name is
"Vous **vous** appelez" = your name is
"Ils/elles **s'**appellent" = their name is

"Comment tu t'appelles?"
What is your name?

"Je m'appelle Charles, et toi?"
My name is Charles, what about you?

"Enchanté!"
Nice to meet you!

"Qui c'est? C'est Amandine."
Who is it? This is Amandine.

"L'AGE" (age)

Whereas English uses the verb "to be" ("être") to speak about the age, French uses the verb "to have" ("avoir").

j'ai	
tu as	
il/elle a	
nous avons	
vous avez	
ils ont	

Note : To refer to somebody's age, we use the French term "un an", whereas we use the French term "une année" to speak about the year.

"**Quel âge** as-tu?" (formal)
"Tu as **quel âge**?" (informal)
How old are you?

"**J'ai** vingt-six ans."
I am 26 years old.

"**Quel âge** elle a?"
How old is she?

"**Elle a** trente ans."
"She is 30 years old.

"LA NATIONALITÉ" (nationality)

When speaking about the nationality ("la nationalité"), you can refer to the country ("le pays") and the city of origin ("la ville"). There is no easy solution to learn the countries and nationalities. The best way is just to learn by heart !

Note : Countries in French are capitalized but there is no capitalization for the nationality or the language.

Below are a few countries/continents and the relevant nationality (notice the ending (e) when you refer to a woman):

Europe : "l'Europe" = "européen(ne)"
France : "la France" = "français(e)"
England : "l'Angleterre" = "anglais(e)"

America : "l'Amérique" = "américain(e)"
USA : "les Etats-Unis" = "américain(e)"
Mexico : "le Mexique" = "mexicain(e)"

Asia : "l'Asie" = "asiatique"

China : "la Chine" = "chinois (e)"
Japan : "le Japon" = "japonais(e)"

Australia : "l'Australie" = "australien(ne)"
New Zealand : "la Nouvelle-Zélande" = "néo-zélandais(e)"

Africa : "l'Afrique" = "africain(e)"
Senegal : "le Sénégal" = "sénégalais(e)"

"De quel pays tu viens?"
What country are you from?

"Je viens de France."
I come from France.

"Quelle est **sa nationalité**?"
What is her nationality?

"Elle est américaine."
She is American.

"LA VILLE D'ORIGINE" (hometown)

Let's speak about your hometown. In French, we speak about "la ville d'origine",
which litterally means "the city of origin".

"habiter à (+ ville)" = to reside in (+ city)
"vivre à (+ ville)" = to live in (+ city)

Where do you live? = "Tu habites où?" (informal)
                     "Où habites-tu?" (formal)

I live in … = "J'**habite à** …"

Examples :
"J'**habite à** Paris." = "Je **vis à** Paris."
I live in Paris.

"Tu **habites à** New-York." = "Tu **vis à** New York."
You live in New York.

"Elle **habite à** Hong-Kong." = "Elle **vit à** Hong-Kong."
She lives in Hong-Kong.

"Nous **habitons à** Berlin." = "Nous **vivons à** Berlin"
We live in Berlin.

"Vous **habitez à** Bueno Aires." = "Vous **vivez à** Bueno Aires."
You live in Bueno Aires.

"Ils **habitent à** Sydney." = "Ils **vivent à** Sydney."
They live in Sydney.

"LA LANGUE" (language)

If you go to France, you need to know how to say that you can or can't speak French! You will use the French verb "parler". Here are a few examples to help you understand how to use it.

"Quelle langue **tu parles**?" or "Quelle langue **parles-tu**?"
What language can you speak?

"**Je parle** français."
I speak French.

"**Elle parle** anglais et espagnol."
She speaks English and Spanish.

"**Nous ne parlons pas** chinois."
We can't speak Chinese.

"LA PROFESSION" (job)

A particularity in French is that some job have a feminine form and some don't. Usually the ones without feminine form were originally physical jobs which were considered as manly work, such as engineers, builders or butchers.

Here is a shortlist of some common jobs :

"un ingénieur" = engineer
"un maçon" = builder
"un boucher" = butcher
"un plombier" = plumber
"un(e) secrétaire" = secretary
"un vendeur / une vendeuse" = salesman/lady
"un(e) comptable" = accountant

"un(e) photographe" = photographer
"un(e) professeur(e)" = teacher
"un étudiant(e)" = student

"Je suis étudiant."
I am a student.

"Elle est ingénieur."
She is an engineer.

"Il est photographe."
He is a photographer.

Speaking about your family

"Les membres de la famille" (family members)

"le père / le papa" = father / dad
"la mère / la maman" = mother / mom
"les parents" = parents
"le mari" = husband
"la femme" = wife
"la fille" = daughter
"le fils" = son
"les enfants" = children
"les petits-enfants" = grandchildren
"le grand-père / le papi" = grandfather / granddad
"la grand-mère / la mamie" = grandmother / grandmom
"le cousin, la cousine" = cousin
"le frère, la soeur" = brother, sister
"un oncle, une tante" = uncle, aunt

Let's practice with a few sentences.

"Mon mari est français."
My husband is French.

"Nous avons deux enfants : un garçon et une fille."
We have two kids : a boy and a girl.

"Quelle est la profession de ton frère? Mon frère est ingénieur."
What is your brother's job? My brother is an engineer.

"Votre femme parle anglais? Non, elle ne parle pas anglais."
Does your wife speak English? No, she doesn't.

"La description physique" (physical aspect)

Let's learn the French words to describe the body parts ("les parties du corps").

"le visage" = face
"la bouche" = mouth
"le nez" = nose
"une oreille, les oreilles" = ear(s)
"un oeil, les yeux" = eye(s)
"les cheveux" = hair
"le bras, les bras" = arm(s)
"la main, les mains" = hand(s)
"un doigt, les doigts" = finger(s)
"une épaule, des épaules" = shoulder(s)
"le dos" = back
"la jambe, les jambes" = leg(s)
"le pied, les pieds" = foot, feet
"un orteil, les orteils" = toe(s)

Let's practice these words on your family now!

"Ma mère a les yeux bleus."
My mother has blue eyes.

"Son grand-père a les yeux verts."
His grand-father has green eyes.

"Ton frère est blond."
Your brother is blond.

"Ma fille a les cheveux marrons."
My daughter has brown hair.

"J'ai un petit nez et un visage rond."
I have a small nose and a round face.

"Il a des bras longs mais des jambes courtes."
He has long arms but short legs.

"Elle porte une écharpe jaune sur l'épaule."

She wears a yellow scarf on the shoulder.

"Tu as le visage très rouge."
Your face is very red.

Note: "les couleurs" (the colors) : "vert" = green; "bleu" = blue; "rouge" = red; "noir" = black; "rose" = pink; "blanc" = white; "orange" = orange; "jaune" = yellow; "gris" = grey; "violet" = purple; "marron" = brown.

"AIMER" (to like)

It can be useful to know how to tell what you like ("aimer") or dislike ("ne pas aimer"), especially when people offer you to taste new food!

"Quelle nourriture **aimes-tu**"
What food do you like?

"**J'aime** le chocolat mais **je n'aime pas** le lait."
I like chocolate but I don't like milk.

"Quelle activité **aime ton père**?"
What activity does your father like?

"**Mon père aime** beaucoup voyager."
My father likes travelling a lot.

"Quel sport **aime ta cousine**?"
What sport does your cousin like?

"**Ta cousine aime** nager et jouer au tennis."
Your cousine likes swimming and playing tennis.

"Test your French!"

Let's review what you've learnt in that chapter with a few exercises.

<u>Mark the correct answers:</u>

"Tu aimes le chocolat?"
□ Oui, j'aime le chocolat.
□ Non, elle n'aime pas le chocolat.
□ Oui, vous aimez le chocolat.

"Quelle est la profession de ton frère?"
☐ Mon frère a les yeux bleus.
☐ Mon père est plombier.
☐ Mon frère est comptable.

"Comment s'appelle ta maman?"
☐ Ma maman a cinquante ans.
☐ Ma maman s'appelle Chantal.
☐ Ma cousine s'appelle Aurélie.

Fill the gaps:

Marie vient des Etats-Unis. Elle est …
Son cousin vit à Berlin. C'est en …
Ce … est … facile de parler français!
Il … Charles et il est étudiant.
Excusez-…, je ne comprends pas!

Translate the sentence:

My grand-father has brown eyes. = ...
Where do you live? We live in Paris. = …
Je vais très bien, et toi? = …
Nous sommes d'accord avec toi = …
My wife likes travelling. = …
Quel âge as-tu? J'ai vingt-deux ans. = …

Answers:

☐ Oui, j'aime le chocolat.
☐ Mon frère est comptable.
☐ Ma maman s'appelle Chantal.

Marie vient des Etats-Unis. Elle est américaine.
Son cousin vit à Berlin. C'est en Allemagne.
Ce n'est pas facile de parler français!
Il s'appelle Charles et il est étudiant.
Excusez-moi, je ne comprends pas!

Mon grand-père a les yeux marrons.
Où habitez-vous? Nous habitons à Paris.
I'm fine, what about you?

We agree with you.
Ma femme aime voyager.
How old are you? I am twenty-two year old.

Chapter 4 : The French "Gourmet" Culture

What you're about to learn:

- ➔ How to approach French cuisine
- ➔ How to enjoy a French meal

Gastronomy & fine food

France is world-renowned as the country of culinary arts. It is indeniable, French food is a must to try. You shoud once immerse yourself in this entire culture to feel how deep and far in history it goes. French cuisine is all about finding exclusive ingredients, using refined techniques and combining pride and mastery to reach the greatest level of gastronomy. French cuisine is about tasting regional products, recognizing the different flavors, in other words a full experience.

"Le fromage" (cheese)

The French consume an average of 45 pounds of cheese per year and per person!

Cheese is on a French table at each meal. There are some 400 different types of regional cheese in France so you can not miss it!

Cheese is classified according to the type of milk it is made of (cow, goat, ewe) and the techniques used (pasteurized, pressed, etc.).

"Le vin" (wine)

Almost every region in France is known for its special cheese and its special wine! To be exact 17 regions out of 22 are wine producers.

French people drink wine on a daily basis along with the meal and they claim its benefits on health! Actually, the French are known to be quite fit so wine might help, right?
France is the number one producer and exporter of wine, which says a lot on French consumption of wine. On average, a French person consumes 1.3 glass of wine per day, which totals to over 50 liters per year. French wine is considered as an art in both ways : producing it and tasting it.

"Le pain" (bread)

Wine, cheese and bread are the three allies of the French! Bread may be the most basic of all kinds of food but it is considered as an institution in France. It is that important that during the French Revolution every French man would consume three pounds of bread daily. If bread supplies ran short or with poor quality, it was a good enough reason for riot!

French bread is only made of four basic ingredients (water, flour, yeast and salt), of which French bakers ("les boulangers français") can create wide varieties of complex breads.

"Les truffes" (truffles)

Although truffles can be found all over the world, French cuisine is known for them. The truffle is a pungent tasting fungus that grows under trees in forested areas. Truffles are expensive as they are quite rare (only to be found in the forest). Only a French Chef knows how to make a divine meal out of a fungus!

"Le foie gras" (foie gras)

Popular delicacy in French cuisine, its flavor is usually described as rich, buttery and delicate. It is made of a liver of a duck or a goose, using a special process as the duck or the goose has been fattened by force-feeding ("le gavage") to make its liver extra big and extra fat.

"Les macarons" (French macarons)

The macarons from *Ladurée* in Paris are well-known around the world and you can now find a *Ladurée* store in Dubai, Hong-Kong, New York or Miami!
The macaron is a sweet meringue-based confection traditionally made with ground almonds, egg whites and sugar. Upon baking, it is filled with ganache, buttercream or jam.

"Les techniques de cuisine françaises"

Many **cooking techniques** have been elaborated by the French. You might already know some of them :

"Flambé" : to cook or finish something by pouring alcohol over it and then lighting it on fire
"Sauté" : cooking something in fat, over high heat
"Blondir" : to lightly brown food in a fat
"Chiffonade" : to cut in thin strips
"Confit" : to cook meat or poultry that is prepared and stored in its own fat

"Gratiné" : to cook in the oven usually topped with cheese

"Emulsion" : to have a lot of fat distributed evenly through a mixture (ex.: mayonnaise)

"Purée" : to obtain a smooth and creamy preparation by the use of a food processor, blender, or by pressing cooked food

All about meals

"L'art du petit-déjeuner" : Breakfast is an art!

Bread and pastry ("le pain et les viennoiseries")

Who hasn't eaten a French baguette before? In France, most people go to the "boulangerie" (bakery) and buy their bread freshly baked everyday.

A few items to select for your own French breakfast :

"le croissant" = croissant
"le pain au chocolat" = chocolate croissant
"la brioche" = brioche
"le pain aux raisins" = raisin bread
"la baguette beurrée" = baguette with butter

"le café au lait" = coffee with milk
"le café crème" = espresso with milk
"le thé au citron" = hot lemon tea
"le chocolat chaud" = hot chocolate
"le jus d'orange" = orange juice

"le beurre" = butter
"la confiture d'abricot" = apricot jam
"la gelée de framboises" = raspberry jelly
"le miel à la lavande" = lavender-flavored honey

"Un déjeuner rapide entre deux clients" : a quick lunch between two clients

Lunch is usually a quick meal in France especially over weekdays. In most restaurants, the "menu du jour" (menu of the day) consists of an entrée, a main dish and/or a dessert and a café.

"le menu du jour" = menu of the day

"la salade au chèvre chaud" = salad with toasted goat cheese

"la salade niçoise" = niçoise salad
"la salade caesar" = caesar salad
"le taboulé" = couscous salad
"le steak-frites" = steak and fries
"l'entrecôte sauce au poivre" = rib steak with pepper sauce
"les pâtes à la carbonara" = pasta with carbonara sauce
"le gratin dauphinois" = potatoe gratin
"la truite aux légumes vapeur" = trout with steamed vegetables
"la ratatouille" = vegetable stew
"l'omelette au fromage et aux lardons" = cheese and bacon omelette

"Un repas sur le pouce" = a meal on the go

"le sandwich jambon-emmental" = ham and cheese sandwich
"le sandwich rosette-cornichons" = sandwich with dried sausage and pickles
"le sandwich au pâté" = sandwich with liver spread
"le sandwich poulet-crudités" = sandwich with chicken and veggies
"la pizza aux quatre fromages" = four cheese pizza
"la pizza végétarienne" = vegetarian pizza
"la crêpe au jambon et au fromage" = thin pancake with ham and cheese
"la crêpe au nutella" = thin pancake with nutella
"la gaufre au sucre" = waffle with sugar

"Le goûter gourmand" : yummy sweet treats

In France, there are as many sweet treats as there are types of wine and cheese! If you go to a bakery or a cake shop, you will be delighted by just looking at the window.

Here are a few samples of a long list of French cakes:

"le chou à la crème" = cream puff pastry
"le clafoutis" = cherries baked in batter
"la bûche de noël" = Christmas cream cake
"une crêpe" = thin pancake
"la crème brûlée" = custard topped with hard caramel
"le far breton" = flan with prunes from Brittany ("la Bretagne")
"le fraisier" = strawberry cream cake
"le baba au rhum" = sponge cake with rhum
"le pain perdu" = French toast
"la galette des rois" = almond tart (epiphany cake)
"les madeleines" = shell-shaped cookies
"le mille-feuille" = puff pastry filled with vanilla cream (supposedly made of a thousand layers!)

"le fondant au chocolat" = chocolate fondant
"la mousse au chocolat" = chocolate mousse
"la tarte aux pommes" = apple pie

"Le dîner par excellence" : the ultimate dinner

In France, the dinner is actually the most important meal of the day. It is not only the most complete but it is also the longest meal. It is the time for the family to gather and talk about the day.

"les entrées" (entree)

"la salade verte" = green leaves salad
"la terrine de légumes" = vegetable terrine
"le pâté de campagne" = country-style pâté
"le pâté de foie" = liver spead
"le pâté en croûte" = meat pie
"le saumon fumé" = smoked salmon
"la soupe de légumes" = vegetable soup
"la soupe à l'oignon" = onion soup

"les viandes" (meat)

"le boeuf" = beef
"le porc" = porc
"le veau" = veal
"le poulet" = chicken
"l'agneau" = lamb

"les poissons" (fish)

"le saumon" = salmon
"la truite" = trout
"la dorade" = sea bream
"la crevette" = shrimp
"le cabillaud" = cod
"la lotte" = monkfish
"le rouget" = red mullet
"le merlan" = whiting
"le thon" = tuna

"Féculents et légumes" (starch and veggies)

"les pâtes" = pasta

"le riz" = rice
"une frite, des frites" = fries
"une pomme de terre, une patate" = potatoe
"un haricot vert" = green bean
"une carotte" = carrot
"un chou-fleur" = cauliflower
"un petit pois" = green pea
"un champignon" = mushroom
"une tomate" = tomatoe
"un oignon" = onion
"l'ail" = garlic

"les fruits" (fruits)

"l'orange" = orange
"le kiwi" = kiwi
"le pamplemousse" = grapefruit
"la fraise" = strawberry
"la mûre" = blackberry
"la pomme" = apple
"la mandarine" = tangerine
"la poire" = pear
"la pêche" = peach
"la cerise" = cherry
"le melon" = melon
"la groseille" = gooseberry
"la prune" = plum

"les condiments" (condiments)

"le sel" = salt
"le poivre" = pepper
"le sucre" = sugar
"les herbes aromatiques" = aromatic herbs
"la moutarde" = mustard
"l'huile" = oil
"le vinaigre" = vinegar
"la vinaigrette" = salad dressing (made of oil and vinegar)
"la farine" = flour

In order to help you set the table, below are the terms used in the kitchen ("la cuisine") and dining room ("la salle à manger").

"mettre le couvert" = to set the table

"la table" = table
"une chaise" = chair
"une assiette" = plate
"un verre" = glass
"une fourchette" = fork
"un couteau" = knife
"une cuillère" = spoon
"une serviette de table" = napkin
"une nappe" = table cloth
"une carafe d'eau" = water pitcher

Dining out

How to make a reservation?

"réserver une table" = to reserve a table
"je voudrais" = I would like

Below are sample sentences aiming at reserving a table in a restaurant.

"Bonjour, je voudrais réserver une table pour samedi soir."
Hello, I'd like to reserve a table for Saturday night.

"Pour combien de personnes?"
For how many?

"Pour quatre personnes."
For 4 people.

"Pour quelle heure?"
At what time?

"A vingt heures."
At 8pm.

"C'est à quel nom?"
What is the name for the reservation?

"Vous préférez à l'intérieur ou à l'extérieur?"
Would you like to seat inside or outside?

"Désolé, le restaurant est fermé/complet ce soir."
Sorry, the restaurant is closed/full tonight.

How to order food and drinks?

At a French restaurant, you can usually chose either the set menu ("le menu") or any other item in the menu ("à la carte").

"l'apéritif" = when you usually get the menu, the waiter/waitress will ask you if you want to start with a drink.

"la carte des vins" = if you want to drink wine, the waiter/waitress will bring the wine list.

"l'entrée" = the "entrée" is the first course refered to as the starter in English.

"le plat principal" = this is the main course, usually meat or fish.

"choisir la cuisson de la viande" = how to select your cooking preferences for meat
"bleu" = blue
"saignant" = rare
"à point" = medium
"bien cuit" = well done

"le fromage" = you have the choice between a selection of dried cheese ("fromage sec") or fresh cheese ("fromage blanc") which usually comes with sugar ("sucre"), sour cream ("crème") or fruit purée ("coulis de fruit"). Some people also chose to eat it with salt and pepper ("sel et poivre").

"la carte des desserts" = dessert menu
"régler l'addition" = to pay the bill
"laisser un pourboire" = to leave a tip

Let's practice!

"Voulez-vous un apéritif?"
What would you like to drink?

"Quel plat recommandez-vous?"
What is your recommendation?

"Je voudrais commander une entrée."
I would like to order a starter.

"En plat principal, vous voulez de la viande ou du poisson?"
Would you like meat or fish for main course?

"Quel accompagnement souhaitez-vous?"
What side dish would you like?

"Quelle sauce voulez-vous avec votre steak?"
What sauce would you like with your steak?

"Vous avez le choix entre la sauce au poivre et la sauce au vin."
You can chose between pepper sauce and wine sauce.

"Souhaitez-vous du fromage sec ou du fromage blanc?"
Would you like dried or fresh cheese?

"Je préfère du fromage blanc."
I prefer fresh cheese.

"Voici la carte des desserts."
Here is the dessert menu.

"Je voudrais l'addition, s'il vous plaît."
I would like the bill, please.

"Est-ce que tout s'est bien passé?"
Was everything alright?

"C'était délicieux! Mes compliments au chef!"
It was delicious! Compliments to the chef!

A drink at the bar

In order to have a drink at the bar, you need to be able to order it, right? Here are a few words and expressions to quench your thirst!

"commander un verre" = to order a drink
"boire un verre" = to have a drink
"commander au bar" = to order at the bar
"laisser un pourboire" = to leave a tip
"la boisson" = the drink

The verb "boire" is irregular so it is important for you to learn its conjugation (present tense):

"je bois" = I drink
"tu bois" = you drink
"il/elle/on boit" = he/she drinks
"nous **buvons**" = we drink
"vous **buvez**" = you drink
"ils/elles **boivent**" = they drink

Below are a few drinks that customers usually order at the bar:

"un verre de vin" = a glass of wine
"un verre de rouge/blanc/rosé" = a glass of red/white/rosé wine
"une bière pression" = draught beer
"une coupe de champagne" = a glass of champagne
"un whisky coca" = whisky coke
"une vodka pomme" = vodka and apple juice
"un demi pêche" = a beer mixed with peach squash
"un panaché" = a beer mixed with limonade
"un pastis" = anise spirit

"Tu bois quoi?" or "Vous buvez quoi?" (familier)
What you drink? (informal)

" Je voudrais un verre de blanc, s'il vous plaît."
I would like a glass of white wine, please."

"On peut commander les boissons?"
Can we order the drinks?"

"On va prendre trois bières pression, merci!"
We will have 3 draught beers, thanks!

"Ca fait 15 euros, s'il vous plaît."
It costs €15, please.

"Test your French!"

Let's review what you've learnt in that chapter with a few exercises.

Mark the correct answers:

"Tu aimes manger quoi au petit-déjeuner?"
□ Une truite aux légumes
□ Du pain avec du beurre et de la confiture

□ Un verre de vin rouge

"Vous avez une table libre pour deux ce soir?"
□ Je suis désolé, le restaurant est fermé ce soir.
□ Le menu du jour coûte quinze euros.
□ Je mange avec mes parents à la maison.

"Vous préférez du fromage blanc ou du fromage sec?"
□ Je bois une bière pression.
□ Nous aimons le fromage.
□ Je préfère du fromage sec.

Fill the gaps:

Voici la ... des desserts.
Je mange un pain … chocolat tous les matins.
Vous préférez à l'... ou à l'extérieur?
Elle aime la ... au poivre et la ... au vin.
Je   ... une coupe de champagne, s'il vous plaît.

Translate the sentence:

Au déjeuner, j'ai mangé des pâtes à la carbonara. = ...
I would like to reserve a table for 4 people. = …
Vous voulez commander les boissons? = …
Il aime manger du fromage et boire du vin. = …
Do you prefer a brioche or a croissant? = …
Le restaurant est complet demain soir? = …

Answers:

□ Du pain avec du beurre et de la confiture
□ Je suis désolé, le restaurant est fermé ce soir.
□ Je préfère du fromage sec.

Voici la carte des desserts.
Je mange un pain au chocolat tous les matins.
Vous préférez à l'extérieur ou à l'extérieur?
Elle aime la sauce au poivre et la sauce au vin.
Je voudrais une coupe de champagne, s'il vous plaît.

I had pasta with carbonara sauce for lunch.
Je voudrais réserver une table pour quatre personnes.

Do you want to order the drinks?
He likes eating cheese and drinking wine.
Tu préfères une brioche ou un croissant?
Is the restaurant full tomorrow night?

Chapter 5 : Travelling Around

What you're about to learn:

→ How to ask for directions
→ How to find transportation
→ How to enjoy the city entertainments
→ How to face an emergency

Locating yourself

Where am I? "Où suis-je?"
Whenever travelling to a new place, you need to be able to locate yourself or ask for the way.

The following location words will be helpful:

"à droite" = on the right
"à gauche" = on the left
"tout droit" = straight
"derrière" = behind
"devant" = in front

"aller" = to go
"avancer" = to go forward
"reculer" = to go backward
"tourner" = to turn
"entrer" = to enter
"sortir" = to exit

"la ruelle" = small street
"l'impasse" = one-way street
"la grande rue, la rue principale" = main street
"le croisement" = intersection
"le centre-ville" = downtown
"la périphérie" = suburbs

Some useful buildings and places to know in a city:

"l'hôtel de ville", "la mairie" = city hall, town hall
"le poste de police" = police station

"la poste" = post office
"la gare" = train station
"l'église" = church
"la place" = square
"le parc" = park
"les jardins publics" = public gardens
"le musée" = museum
"une école" = school
"un lycée" = highschool
"une université" = university

Asking questions and expressions to get help finding your way:

"Où suis-je?"
Where am I?

"Pouvez-vous me montrer sur le plan?"
Can you show me on the map?

"Allez tout droit et tournez à gauche."
Go straight and then turn to the left.

"Je suis perdu. Pouvez-vous m'aider, s'il vous plaît?"
I am lost. Can you help me, please?

"Où allez-vous?"
Where do you go?

"Je veux aller à la poste."
I want to go to the post office.

"Pouvez-vous m'indiquer la mairie, s'il vous plaît?"
Can you tell me where the city hall is?

"Je cherche le centre commercial."
I am looking for the shopping mall.

"C'est dans quelle rue?"
In which street is it?

"C'est au numéro trois de la rue du Général de Gaulle."
It is located at the number three on Général de Gaulle street.

Transportation

Upon your arrival in a French city, you usually have several transportation options. You can use private transportation such a taxi or renting a car, or public transportation, such as the bus, the train, the subway.

We will give you a minimum of vocabulary and expressions to be able to use either one of this transportation means.

"LE TAXI"

"prendre le taxi" = hiring a taxi
"le chauffeur de taxi" = taxi driver
"ouvrir le coffre" = to open the trunk
"ouvrir la porte" = to open the door
"la valise" = suitcase
"le sac à dos = backpack
"mettre le compteur" = to start the meter
"aller à" = to go
"s'arrêter" = to stop
"le tarif" = rate

"Où sont les taxis, s'il vous plaît?"
Where are the taxis, please?

"Pouvez-vous m'appeler un taxi, s'il vous plaît?"
Can you call a taxi for me, please?

"Pouvez-vous mettre ma valise dans le coffre, s'il vous plaît?"
Can you put my suitcase in the trunk, please?

"Où allez-vous?"
Where do you go?

"Je vais à l'hôtel Mercure, trois rue de la Résistance."
I am going to Mercure Hotel, number 3 on Résistance street.

"Combien je vous dois?"
How much do I owe you?

"Arrêtez-vous, c'est ici!"
Stop, it's here!

"LE TRAIN"

"prendre le train" = to take the train
"aller à la gare" = to go to the train station
"le guichet" = ticket window
"le quai" = platform
"acheter/prendre un billet" = to buy a ticket
"un aller-simple" = one-way trip
"un aller-retour" = round trip
"les horaires de train" = train timetable
"voyager en première/deuxième classe" = to travel first/second class
"une place réservée" = reserved seat
"le numéro de place" = seat number
"la place côté couloir/fenêtre" = the seat next to the aisle/window
"la consigne à bagages" = baggage lockers
"le bureau des objets trouvés" = lost-and-found
"la salle d'attente" = waiting room
"changer de train" = to change trains
"avoir une correspondance" = to have a connecting train
"le contrôleur" = inspector
"monter dans le train" = to get in the train
"descendre du train" = to get off the train

"Où pouvons-nous acheter les tickets?"
Where can we buy the tickets?

"Avez-vous les horaires du train pour Paris?"
Do you have the timetable of the train to Paris?

"Je voudrais un aller-retour pour Marseille, s'il vous plaît."
I would like a round trip ticket to go to Marseille, please.

"Combien coûte le billet?"
How much is the ticket?

"Je dois changer de train à Aix-en-Provence."
I have to change trains in Aix-en-Provence.

"De quel quai part le train?"
From which platform does the train leave?

"Pouvez-vous m'aider à mettre ma valise dans le train, s'il vous plaît?"
Could you help me put my suitcase in the train, please?

"Où est le wagon restaurant?"
Where is the food car?

"LE BUS"

"prendre le bus" = to take the bus
"la ligne de bus" = bus line
"l'arrêt de bus" = bus stop
"le chauffeur de bus" = bus driver
"acheter un billet de bus" = to buy a bus ticket
"composter le billet" = to validate the ticket
"monter dans le bus" = to get in the bus
"descendre du bus" = to get off the bus
"demander l'arrêt du bus" = to ask for the bus to stop

"Excusez-moi, c'est le bus en direction du centre-ville?"
Excuse-me, is it the bus going downtown?

"Je dois prendre la ligne de bus numéro 15."
I have to take the bus line number 15.

"C'est à combien d'arrêts d'ici?"
How many stops is it from here?

"Le bus passe à quelle heure?"
What time will the bus arrive?

"LE METRO"

"prendre le métro" = to take the subway
"la station de métro" = subway station
"acheter un ticket de métro" = to buy a subway ticket
"le plan du métro" = subway map
"la ligne de métro" = subway line
"monter dans le métro" = to get in the subway
"descendre du métro" = to get off the subway

"Quelle est la ligne directe pour aller à Montmartre?"
What is the direct line to go to Montmartre?

"Où se trouve l'entrée/la sortie du métro?"
Where is the subway entrance/exit?

"Je voudrais acheter un ticket de métro, s'il vous plaît."
I would like to buy a subway ticket, please.

"Vous devez descendre à l'arrêt Champs-Elysées."
You have to get off at Champs-Elysées.

"LA VOITURE DE LOCATION"

"la voiture de location" = rental car
"louer une voiture" = to rent a car
"rendre la voiture" = to return the car
"conduire une voiture" = to drive a car
"l'agence de location de voitures" = rental car company
"faire le plein" = to fill up the tank
"le carburant" = fuel
"le sans-plomb" = unleaded fuel
"le diesel" = diesel fuel
"les clés de la voiture" = car keys
"le permis de conduire" = driving licence
"l'assurance de la voiture" = car insurance

"Nous voulons louer une voiture, s'il vous plaît."
We would like to rent a car, please.

"Combien ça coûte pour dix jours de location?"
How much is the rate for ten days rental ?

"Nous n'avons pas besoin d'assurance. Nous avons une assurance tous risques avec notre carte de crédit."
We don't need insurance. We have full insurance with our credit card.

"Dans quel pays voulez-vous conduire?"
In what country do you want to drive?

"Il faut mettre du sans-plomb."
You have to use unleaded.

"Voici le numéro pour le dépannage en cas d'accident."
Here is the phone number for towing in case of an accident.

Fun in town

When visiting a new place, it is fun to try out local entertainment. Here are some words and expressions that will help you enjoy every bit of the journey!

First you can start by visiting a few **museums** ("le musée") to get a grasp of local culture. Especially if you are travelling to Paris, you should not miss its amazing museums : le Musée du Louvre, le Château de Versailles, le Musée d'Orsay, etc.

"visiter un musée" = to visit a museum
"acheter un billet d'entrée" = to buy an entrance ticket
" la carte de réduction" = discount card
"le guide" = guidebook
"photos (au flash) interdites" = no (flash) photography
"défense d'entrée" = no admittance

"Combien coûte le billet d'entrée du musée?"
How much is the museum entrance ticket?

"Le billet plein tarif/demi tarif coûte dix euros."
The full price/half price ticket costs 10 Euros.

"Quand est la prochaine visite guidée?"
When is the next guided tour?

"La visite guidée commence dans dix minutes."
The guided tour starts in ten minutes.

French theater ("le théâtre") is famous around the world and you can find shows at every price for every taste. We advise you to make reservations if you want to attend one of the national theaters. In small local theaters you can get last minute tickets at the door. Formal outfit is usually expected when going to a theater or to the opera in big cities.

"la pièce de théâtre" = the theater show
"la comédie" = comédie
"le drame" = drama
"l'entracte" = intermission
"une place à l'orchestre" = orchestra seat
"le balcon" = balcony
"complet" = sold out
"le lever de rideau" = the curtain goes up

You might want to try the **movies** ("le cinéma") to test how much your French has improved. However don't expect to find too many English movies showing in their original version. International movies showing in French are very often French versions.

"aller au cinéma" = to go to the movies

"regarder un film" = to watch a movie
"la version originale" (VO) = original version
"la version française" (VF) = French version
"les sous-titres" = subtitles
"le film d'aventure" = adventure movie
"la comédie romantique" = romance
"le dessin animé" = cartoon
"le film d'horreur" = horror movie
"le film policier" = suspense movie

After a day embracing French culture, you might want to get wild at the **nightclub** ("la boîte") and enjoy lively night life with French fellows! Don't forget to dress up, the French are pretty fancy especially in Paris and big cities.

"aller en boîte" = to go to the nightclub
"aller danser" = to go dancing
"faire la queue à l'entrée" = to queue at the door
"l'entrée avec une consommation gratuite" = the ticket with one free drink
"gratuit pour les filles le jeudi soir" = free entrance for girls every Thursday

Last but not least, *when in Rome shop like the Romans!* **Shopping** ("faire les magasins") has indeed its own importance in French cultural life. You will definitely enjoy local markets, little stores, fancy boutiques or big shopping malls.

"le magasin" = store
"acheter" = to buy
"vendre" = to sell
"payer" = to pay
"faire les magasins" = to shop
"le centre commercial" = shopping mall
"la librairie" = bookstore
"la bijouterie" = jewelry store
"la boutique de vêtements" = clothing store
"le marché" = market
"les horaires d'ouverture/de fermeture" = opening/closing hours
"passer à la caisse" = to go to the cash register
"les soldes" = sales
"la vendeuse/le vendeur" = saleslady/salesman
"la cabine d'essayage" = fitting room
"la taille" = size
"la pointure" = shoe size

"Combien ça coûte?"
How much it it?

"A quelle heure le magasin ouvre?"
At what time does the store open?

"Je peux essayer cette robe?"
Can I try on this dress?

"Vous prenez la carte de crédit?"
Do you take credit card?

"Avez-vous de la monnaie, s'il vous plaît?"
Do you have change, please?

"Pouvez-vous m'aider? Je cherche un livre sur le vin."
Can you help me? I'm looking for a book about wine.

Facing emergencies

Whether you get involved into an accident or you witness one and want to help out, you need the minimum of French vocabulary to get through it.

Below are several lists of French words and expressions which apply to different types of circumstances. We will try to cover every scenario possible to help you getting ready to face anything in French!

"L'accident" (accident)

"perdre connaissance" = to be unconscious
"tomber" = to fall
"respirer/ne pas respirer" = breathing/no breathing
"être blessé, avoir mal" = to be hurt
"souffrir" = to suffer
"saigner" = to bleed
"faire une crise cardiaque" = to have a heart attack

"Les secours" (emergency services)

"l'hôpital" = hospital
"le médecin" = doctor
"les urgences" = emergency room
"la police" = police
"les pompiers" = firefighters
"appeler une ambulance" = to call for an ambulance

"le numéro des urgences" = emergency phone number

"Demander de l'aide" (asking for help)

"A l'aide!", "Au secours!"
Help!

"Au feu!"
Fire!

"Pouvez-vous appeler un médecin/les urgences?"
Can you call a doctor/911?

"Pouvez-vous m'aider?"
Can you help me?

"Cette femme est blessée."
This woman is hurt.

"Il a perdu connaissance et il ne respire plus."
He fainted and doesn't breathe.

"Il saigne beaucoup, il faut l'emmener à l'hôpital."
He's bleeding a lot, we have to take him to hospital.

"Ne bougez-pas!"
Don't move!

"Où avez-vous mal?"
Where does it hurt?

"J'ai mal à la jambe/au bras."
My leg/arm hurts.

"A l'hôpital" (at the hospital)

"faire une analyse de sang" = to do a blood test
"faire une radio" = to take an X-ray
"une fracture" = fracture
"une coupure" = cut
"une brûlure" = burn
"poser un plâtre" = to get a cast
"faire un pansement" = to bandage a wound
"recoudre une plaie" = to get stitches

"être cardiaque" = to have a heart condition
"être diabétique" = to be diabetic
"avoir de l'hypertension" = to have high blood pressure
"être allergique à un médicament" = to be allergic to a medicine
"prendre un traitement" = to take a medication

"A la pharmacie" (at the drugstore)

"être enrhumé" = to have a cold
"avoir mal à la gorge" = to have a sore throat
"le mal de tête" = headache
"avoir la diarrhée" = to have diarrhea
"être constipé" = to be constipated
"une allergie" = allergy
"le médicament" = medicine

"De quoi souffrez-vous?"
What are you suffering from?

"J'ai mal à la gorge et je suis enrhumé."
I have a sore throat and a cold.

"Avez-vous un médicament contre les migraines?"
Do you have a medication against migraines?

"Test your French!"

Let's review what you've learnt in that chapter with a few exercises.

Mark the correct answers:

"Où allez-vous?"
□ J'ai mal au pied.
□ Elle veut essayer une robe.
□ Nous allons à la poste.

"A quelle heure le magasin ouvre?"
□ Je cherche un livre sur le vin.
□ Le magasin ouvre à dix heures le matin.
□ Anne a acheté du fromage au magasin d'alimentation.

"Tu as déjà acheté ton billet de train?"
□ Non, je n'ai pas encore acheté mon billet de train.

□ Elle prend le train pour Marseille samedi prochain.
□ Je voudrais deux billets pour Paris, s'il vous plaît.

Fill the gaps:

Excusez-moi, vous prenez la ... de crédit?
Pouvez-vous me ... la gare sur le plan, s'il vous plaît?
Je veux ... au cinéma avec mon frère.
L'homme a perdu ... et il ne respire plus.
Je voudrais un ... contre le mal de gorge.

Translate the sentence:

L'hôtel de ville est à droite de la place.
Go straight and then turn to the right.
Je cherche le quai du train pour Lille.
Au cinéma, il y des films en version française.
My arm hurts and I can not breathe!
Elle est blessée, appelez une ambulance!

Answers:

□ Nous allons à la poste.
□ Le magasin ouvre à dix heures le matin.
□ Non, je n'ai pas encore acheté mon billet de train.

Excusez-moi, vous prenez la carte de crédit?
Pouvez-vous me montrer la gare sur le plan, s'il vous plaît?
Je veux aller au cinéma avec mon frère.
L'homme a perdu connaissance et il ne respire plus.
Je voudrais un médicament contre le mal de gorge.

The city hall is on the right of the square.
Allez tout droit et tournez à droite.
I am looking for the platform of the train to Lille.
At the movie theater there are movies in French version.
J'ai mal au bras et je ne peux pas respirer!
She is hurt, call an ambulance!

Chapter 6 : Business Matters

What you're about to learn:

- → How to get familiar with the French workplace
- → How to arrange business meetings and calls
- → How to successfully plan a business trip

The workplace

Whether you are planning to settle down or go on a business trip to France, you need to know how to navigate the French workplace. You will learn here a few words and expressions to become more familiar.

"une entreprise" = company
"le chef d'entreprise/le PDG" = manager/CEO
"le/la secrétaire" = secretary
"le bureau" = office, desk
"travailler" = to work
"la profession" = job
"conduire un projet/une mission" = to run a project/mission
"le chiffre d'affaire" = turnover
"le salaire" = salary, income
"faire une présentation à un client" = to make a presentation to a client
"signer un contrat" = to sign a contract
"le rendez-vous d'affaire" = business meeting
"la salle de réunion" = conference room
"organiser/diriger une réunion de travail" = to organize/conduct a business meeting/conference
"le(s) document(s) de travail" = working document(s)
"envoyer par courrier électronique" = to send by email
"faire une photocopie" = to copy
"scanner" = to scan
"faxer" = to fax

Doing business

Doing business in France implies to know how to properly meet your clients or counterparts. Indeed, first impressions are extremely important for the French and it might totally ruin your project. Remember to use the formal speech as a mark of respect : "vous" instead of "tu".

Answering the phone in French is rather easy. Greetings will be done via two words : "allô bonjour" (hello in English). Introducing is usually as follows: "Marie à l'appareil" (Marie speaking).

"Au téléphone" (on the phone)

"sonner" = to ring
"décrocher/raccrocher le téléphone" = to pick up/hang up the phone
"répondre au téléphone" = to answer the phone
"l'appel téléphonique" = phone call
"parler (plus) lentement/vite" = speak (more) slowly/fast
"parler (plus) doucement/fort" = speak (more) softly/loudly
"laisser/prendre un message" = to leave/take a message
"rappeler plus tard" = to call back later
"être absent/indisponible/occupé" = to be absent/unavailable/busy
"rester en ligne" = to hold the line
"patienter/attendre un instant" = to wait for a while
"laisser un message sur le répondeur" = to leave a voicemail

"Un exemple d'appel téléphonique" (a phone call example):

"Entreprise Michard. Marie à l'appareil."
"Michard Corporation. Marie speaking."

"Bonjour Madame, je suis Mademoiselle Martin. Je souhaite parler à Monsieur Michard."
"Good morning, Mrs. I am Miss Martin. I would like to talk to Mr. Michard."

"Bonjour Mademoiselle. Patientez un instant, je vérifie s'il peut vous répondre."
"Good morning Miss. Wait for a while, I will check if he is able to answer."

"Monsieur Michard est occupé actuellement. Je peux prendre un message?"
"Mr Michard is busy right now. Can I take a message?"

"Non, merci. Je rappelerai plus tard. Au revoir Madame."
"No thank you. I will call back later. Good bye Mrs."

"Très bien. Je vous souhaite une bonne journée, Mademoiselle."
"Alright. Have a good day, Miss."

"Le rendez-vous d'affaires" (business meeting)

"prendre rendez-vous" = to schedule an appointment

"consulter le calendrier" = to check the calendar
"fixer une date/un lieu de rendez-vous" = to set up a date/place of meeting
"être disponible/libre" = to be available/free
"ne pas être disponible", "être pris", "être occupé" = to be busy
"être absent" = to be absent
"se rencontrer" = to meet
"conclure une affaire" = to close a deal
"un accord" = an agreement
"être d'accord" = to agree
"le déjeuner d'affaires" = business lunch
"la poignée de main" = handshake
"marché conclu!" = deal!

Planning a business trip

When going on a business trip, it is important to find a good hotel to get the rest you need to close successful deals! Here are some useful words and expressions to be used at the hotel.

"Le voyage d'affaires" (business trip)

"faire un voyage d'affaires" = to go on a business trip
"la chambre d'hôtel" = hotel room
"réserver une chambre" = to book a room
"complet" = fully booked
"la réception" = front desk
"s'enregistrer à la réception" = to register at the front desk
"remplir la fiche d'enregistrement" = to fill up the registration form
"libérer la chambre" = to check out
"payer/régler la note d'hôtel" = to pay the hotel bill
"demander un reçu" = to ask for a receipt
"le petit-déjeuner inclus/exclus" = breakfast included/excluded
"la demi-pension" = half-board
"la pension complète" = full-board
"la chambre double" = double room
"les lits jumeaux" = twin beds
"les toilettes" = restroom

"Je voudrais réserver une chambre pour deux personnes."
I would like to book a room for two.

"C'est pour deux nuits, du 15 au 17 juin."
For two nights, June 15th to 17th.

"C'est combien la nuit?"
How much is it a night?

"Avez-vous une salle de conférence à l'hôtel?"
Do you have a conference room at the hotel?

"Veuillez remplir la fiche d'enregistrement, s'il vous plaît."
Please fill up the registration form.

"Vous devez libérer la chambre à midi."
You have to check out at noon.

"L'ascenseur est à gauche au bout du couloir."
The elevator is on your left at the end of the hall.

"Vous pouvez laisser vos bagages à la réception."
You can leave your luggage at the front desk.

"Le petit-déjeuner est servi entre six heures et dix heures."
Breakfast is served between 6am and 10am.

"Test your French!"

Let's review what you've learnt in that chapter with a few exercises.

Mark the correct answers:

"A qui souhaitez-vous parler?"
☐ Oui, je parle avec la secrétaire.
☐ Je souhaite parler à Monsieur Marcel.
☐ Non, elle n'est pas disponible.

"Quelle chambre souhaitez-vous réserver?"
☐ Je voudrais réserver une chambre double.
☐ Je voudrais un petit-déjeuner demain.
☐ Nous n'avons plus de chambre libre.

"Quand êtes-vous disponible pour prendre rendez-vous?"
☐ Elle n'est pas disponible demain.
☐ Je suis disponible mardi à 15h.
☐ Nous avons réservé une chambre pour deux.

Fill the gaps:

Ma secrétaire va organiser … réunion de travail demain.
Vous pouvez laisser vos bagages à la … .
Patientez … …, je vérifie si Monsieur Albert est disponible.
Non, je ne veux pas une … double, c'est pour une personne.
Nous sommes contents, nous allons … une affaire.

Translate the sentence:

C'est combien la nuit? = …
Good morning, I would like to talk to Mrs. Sophie, please. = …
Je voudrais réserver une chambre pour deux personnes. = …
Quand as-tu organisé la réunion de travail? = …
I am sorry, I am not available right now. = ...
Do you want to leave your luggage at the front desk? = ...

Answers:

□ Je souhaite parler à Monsieur Marcel.
□ Je voudrais réserver une chambre double.
□ Je suis disponible mardi à 15h.

Ma secrétaire va organiser la réunion de travail demain.
Vous pouvez laisser vos bagages à la réception.
Patientez un instant, je vérifie si Monsieur Albert est disponible.
Non, je ne veux pas une chambre double, c'est pour une personne.
Nous sommes contents, nous allons conclure une affaire.

How much is it a night?
Bonjour, je souhaite parler à Madame Sophie, s'il vous plaît.
I would like to book a room for two.
When did you organize the business conference/meeting?
Je suis désolé, je ne suis pas disponible actuellement.
Voulez-vous laisser vos bagages à la réception?

Chapter 7 : All About Numbers

What you're about to learn:

- → How to properly use ordinal and cardinal numbers
- → How to tell the time and the date
- → How to use numbers to talk about money

Let's count

You may need only to know numbers from 0 ("zéro") to 100 ("cent") to be able to count your money left, the number of documents you have to sign, the amount of gifts you will bring home... or to tell the time!

Ordinal numbers ("les nombres ordinaux")

1	un	20	vingt	39	trente-neuf
2	deux	21	vingt-et-un	40	quarante
3	trois	22	vingt-deux	41	quarante-et-un
4	quatre	23	vingt-trois	42	quarante-deux
5	cinq	24	vingt-quatre	50	cinquante
6	six	25	vingt-cinq	51	cinquante-et-un
7	sept	26	vingt-six	60	soixante
8	huit	27	vingt-sept	61	soixante-et-un
9	neuf	28	vingt-huit	70	soixante-dix
10	dix	29	vingt-neuf	71	soixante-et-onze
11	onze	30	trente	72	soixante-douze
12	douze	31	trente-et-un	80	quatre-vingt
13	treize	32	trente-deux	81	quatre-vingt-un
14	quatorze	33	trente-trois	90	quatre-vingt-dix
15	quinze	34	trente-quatre	91	quatre-vingt-onze
16	seize	35	trente-cinq	92	quatre-vingt-douze
17	dix-sept	36	trente-six	100	cent

18	dix-huit	37	trente-sept	101	cent-un
19	dix-neuf	38	trente-huit	102	cent-deux

Cardinal numbers ("les nombres cardinaux")

"premier" : first
"deuxième" : second
"troisième" : third
"quatrième" : fourth
"cinquième" : fifth
"sixième : sixth
"septième" : seventh
"huitième" : eighth
"neuvième" : ninth
"dizième" : tenth

A few sentences to practise cardinal numbers:

"Elle est arrivée **la première** à la maison."
She was the first to arrive at home.

"C'est **la troisième fois** que tu es en retard!"
You are late for the third time!"

"Il est **huitième** sur trente à l'école."
He is ranked eight out of thirty at school.

The clock is ticking

"Les sept jours de la semaine" (7 days in a week)

"lundi" = Monday
"mardi" = Tuesday
"mercredi" = Wednesday
"jeudi" = Thursday
"vendredi" = Friday
"samedi" = Saturday
"dimanche" = Sunday

"Les douze mois de l'année" (12 months in a year)

"janvier" = January
"février" = February
"mars" = March
"avril" = April
"mai" = May
"juin" = June
"juillet" = July
"août" = August
"septembre" = September
"octobre" = October
"novembre" = November
"décembre" = December

"Les vingt-quatre heures d'une journée" (24 hours in a day)

midnight = "minuit"
1am = "une heure"
2am = "deux heures"
3am = "trois heures"
4am = "quatre heures"
5am = "cinq heures"
6am = "six heures"
7am = "sept heures"
8am = "huit heures"
9am = "neuf heures"
10am = "dix heures"
11am = "onze heure"
midday = "midi"
1pm = "treize heures"
2pm = "quatorze heures"
3pm = "quinze heures"
4pm = "seize heures"
5pm = "dix-sept heures"
6pm = "dix-huit heures"
7pm = "dix-neuf heures"
8pm = "vingt heures"
9pm = "vingt et une heures"
10pm = "vingt-deux heures"
11pm = "vingt-trois heures"

"Comment donner la date et l'heure?"
(How to tell the date and the time?)

"Quelle est la date aujourd'hui?" or "Quel jour c'est?"
What's the date today?

"Aujourd'hui, c'est lundi 14 avril."
Today is Monday, April 14th.

"C'est le combien demain?" or "On sera le combien demain?"
What's the date tomorrow?

"Demain, c'est mardi 15 avril."
Tomorrow will be Tuesday, April 15th.

"Vous avez l'heure?"
Do you have the time?

"Quelle heure est-il?"
What time is it?

It's 9:30am = "Il est neuf heures trente."
It's 11:40am =   "Il est onze heure quarante."
It's 4:10pm = "Il est seize heures dix."
It's 8:15pm = "Il est vingt heures quinze."

How much money?

"coûter" = to cost
"changer/retirer de l'argent" = to exhange/withdraw money
"la banque" = bank
"le distributeur" = ATM
"insérer/retirer la carte" = to insert/take the card
"taper le code" = enter the PIN

Below are a few sentences which could be useful when dealing with money and banking matters.

"Combien ça coûte?"
Ca coûte cinquante euros.

"Bonjour, je peux pous aider?"
Hello, can I help you?

"Je voudrais changer cinq cent dollars en euros."
I would like to change USD 500 in Euros.

"Quel est le taux de change?"
What is the exchange rate?

"Où est le distributeur le plus proche, s'il vous plaît?"
Where is the closest ATM, please?

"Excusez-moi, le distributeur a avalé ma carte!"
Excuse-me, the ATM machine just swallowed my credit card!

"Test your French!"

Let's review what you've learnt in that chapter with a few exercises.

Mark the correct answers:

"Quelle heure est-il?"
□ Oui, il est en retard.
□ Il est deux heures dix.
□ Ce n'est pas l'heure.

"Quel jour c'est aujourd'hui?"
□ Je vais à Paris mardi matin.
□ Demain, c'est dimanche 20 juin.
□ Mardi 25 novembre.

"Combien coûte le billet de train?"
□ J'ai la place numéro trente-trois.
□ Le billet coûte vingt-cinq euros.
□ Nous avons acheté trois billets de train.

Fill the gaps:

Entre janvier et mars, il y a le mois de … .
Je dois retirer de l'… à la banque.
Un billet de train pour Paris … cinquante euros.
Dans une semaine, il y a … jours.
A quelle … tu as rendez-vous demain?

Translate the sentence:

It's 8:45am. = …

C'est la première fois que je suis en retard. = …
Je vais à l'école du lundi au vendredi. = …
A quelle heure est ton train demain? = …
I would like to change €250 in USD. = …
Insérer la carte et taper le code. = ...

Answers:

☐ Il est deux heures dix.
☐ Mardi 25 novembre.
☐ Le billet coûte vingt-cinq euros.

Entre janvier et mars, il y a le mois de février.
Je dois retirer de l'argent à la banque.
Un billet de train pour Paris coûte cinquante euros.
Dans une semaine, il y a sept jours.
A quelle heure tu as rendez-vous demain?

Il est neuf heures moins le quart.
It's the first time that I'm late.
I go to school from Monday to Friday.
What time is your train tomorrow?
Je voudrais changer deux cent cinquante euros en dollars.
Insert the card and enter the PIN.

Conclusion

Now, Embark on Your Own Adventure!

Now you are ready to go out there and start communicating in the basic French that you have learned from this book. Keep in mind that you have not learned how to say *everything* in French, but you are equipped to make a great start and work your way around using what you now know. Don't forget the basic language skills that you have learned in this book. If you don't know how to say something, ask, use context clues, describe it using the language that you know, and you will eventually find the answer.

Don't worry about looking silly and just do your best to learn from the mistakes you make! Keep a journal to write about your experiences and the new things that you are learning every day. Though it's not always easy and sometimes rather frustrating, traveling abroad is one of the most rewarding experiences you will have. I hope this book has prepared you well and wish you many exciting and fulfilling adventures in your travels!

To your success,

Dagny Taggart

Preview Of "Learn Spanish In 7 DAYS! - The Ultimate Crash Course To Learn The Basics of the Spanish Language In No Time"

Are You ready? It's Time To Learn Spanish!

Most people are daunted by the idea of learning a language. They think it's impossible, even unfathomable. I remember as a junior in high school, watching footage of Jackie O giving a speech in French. I was so impressed and inspired by the ease at which she spoke this other language of which I could not understand one single word.

At that moment, I knew I had to learn at least one foreign language. I started with Spanish, later took on Mandarin, and most recently have started learning Portuguese. No matter how challenging and unattainable it may seem, millions of people have done it. You do NOT have to be a genius to learn another language. You DO have to be willing to take risks and make mistakes, sometimes even make a fool of yourself, be dedicated, and of course, practice, practice, practice!

This book will only provide you with the basics in order to get started learning the Spanish language. It is geared towards those who are planning to travel to a Spanish-speaking country and covers many common scenarios you may find yourself in so feel free to skip around to the topic that is most prudent to you at the moment. It is also focused on the Spanish of Latin America rather than Spain. Keep in mind, every Spanish-speaking country has some language details specific to them so it would be essential to do some research on the specific country or countries that you will visit.

I will now list some tips that I have found useful and should be very helpful to you in your journey of learning Spanish. I don't wish you luck because that will not get you anywhere- reading this book, dedicating yourself, and taking some risks will!

Important note

Due to the nature of this book (it contains charts, graphs, and so on), you will better your reading experience by setting your device on *LANDSCAPE* mode! (In case you're using an electronic device like Kindle).

Language Tips

Tip #1 - Keep an Open Mind

It may seem obvious but you must understand that languages are very different from each other. You cannot expect them to translate word for word. '*There is a black dog*' will not translate word for word with the same word order in Spanish. You have to get used to the idea of translating WHOLE ideas. So don't find yourself saying, "*Why is everything backwards in Spanish?*" because it may seem that way many times.   Keep your mind open to the many differences that you will find in the language that go far beyond just the words.

Tip #2 - Take Risks

Be fearless. Talk to as many people as you can. The more practice you get the better and don't worry about looking like a fool when you say, "*I am pregnant*" rather than "*I am embarrassed*," which as you will find out can be a common mistake. If anyone is laughing remember they are not laughing at you. Just laugh with them, move on, and LEARN from it, which brings us to our next tip.

Tip #3 - Learn from your Mistakes

It doesn't help to get down because you made one more mistake when trying to order at a restaurant, take a taxi, or just in a friendly conversation. Making mistakes is a HUGE part of learning a language. You have to put yourself out there as we said and be willing to make tons of mistakes! Why? Because what can you do with mistakes. You can LEARN from them. If you never make a mistake, you probably are not learning as much as you could. So every time you mess up when trying to communicate, learn from it, move on, and keep your head up!

Tip #4 - Immerse yourself in the language

If you're not yet able to go to a Spanish-speaking country, try to pretend that you are. Surround yourself with Spanish. Listen to music in Spanish, watch movies, TV shows, in Spanish. Play games on your phone, computer, etc. in Spanish. Another great idea is to actually put your phone, computer, tablet and/or other electronic devices in Spanish. It can be frustrating at first but in the end this exposure will definitely pay off.

Tip #5 - Start Thinking in Spanish

I remember being a senior in high school and working as a lifeguard at a fairly deserted pool. While I was sitting and staring at the empty waters, I would speak to myself or think to myself (to not seem so crazy) in Spanish. I would describe my surroundings, talk about what I had done and what I was going to do, etc.

While I was riding my bike, I would do the same thing. During any activity when you don't need to talk or think about anything else, keep your brain constantly going in Spanish to get even more practice in the language. So get ready to turn off the English and jumpstart your Spanish brain!

Tip #6 - Label your Surroundings/Use Flashcards

When I started to learn Portuguese, I bought an excellent book that included stickers so that you could label your surroundings. So I had stickers all over my parents' house from the kitchen to the bathroom that labeled the door, the dishes, furniture, parts of the house, etc. It was a great, constant reminder of how to say these objects in another language. You can just make your own labels and stick them all over the house and hope it doesn't bother your family or housemates too much!

Tip #7 - Use Context clues, visuals, gestures, expressions, etc.

If you don't understand a word that you have heard or read, look or listen to the surrounding words and the situation to help you. If you are in a restaurant and your friend says, "I am going to ??? a sandwich." You can take a guess that she said *order* or *eat* but you don't have to understand every word in order to understand the general meaning. When you are in a conversation use gestures, expressions, and things around you to help communicate your meaning. Teaching English as a second language to young learners taught me this. If you act everything out, you are more likely to get your point across. If you need to say the word *bird* and you don't know how you can start flapping your arms and chirping and then you will get your point across and possibly learn how to say *bird*. It may seem ridiculous but as I said, you have to be willing to look silly to learn another language and this greatly helps your language communication and learning.

Tip #8 - Circumlocution

Circumlo… what? This is just a fancy word for describing something when you don't know how to say it.   If you are looking to buy an umbrella and don't know how to say it, what can you do? You can describe it using words you know. You can say, it is something used for the rain that opens and closes and then hopefully someone will understand you, help you, and maybe teach you how to say this word. Using circumlocution is excellent language practice and is much better than just giving up when you don't know how to say a word. So keep talking even if you have a limited vocabulary. Say what you can and describe or act out what you can't!

SECTION 1: THE BASICS

Chapter 1: Getting the Pronunciation Down

Below I will break down general Spanish pronunciation for the whole alphabet dividing it into vowels and consonants. One great thing about Spanish is that the letters almost always stay consistent as far as what sound they make. Unlike English in which the vowels can make up to 27 different sounds depending on how they are mixed. Be thankful that you don't have to learn English or at least have already learned English. There are of course some sounds in Spanish that we never make in English and you possibly have never made in your life. So get ready to start moving your mouth and tongue in a new way that may seem strange at first but as I keep saying, practice makes perfect!

The charts on the next page will explain how to say the letter, pronounce it, and if there is an example in an English word of how to say it I put it in the right column.

Vowel Sounds

Vowel	How to say the letter	How to pronounce it in a word	As in...
a	Ah	Ah	Taco
e	Eh	Eh	Egg
i	Ee	Ee	Easy
o	Oh	Oh	Open
u	Oo	Oo	Book

Consonant Sounds

Consonant	How to say the letter	How to pronounce it in a word	As in...
b	beh	similar to English b	
c	ceh	k after *a, o,* or *u* s after *e* or *i*	cat cereal
ch	cheh	ch	cheese
d	deh	a soft d (place your	three

		tongue at the back of your upper teeth)	
f	efe	F	free
g	geh	h before i or e g before a, o, u	him go
h	ache	silent	
j	hota	H	him
k	kah	K	karaoke
l	ele	like English l with tongue raised to roof of mouth	
ll	eye	Y	yes
m	eme	M	money
n	ene	N	no
ñ	enye	Ny	canyon
p	peh	like English p but you don't aspirate	

Consonants continued

Consonant	How to say the letter	How to pronounce it in a word	As in…
Q	koo	k (q is always followed by u like English)	quilt
R	ere	* at the beginning of a word you must roll your r's by vibrating tongue at roof of mouth * in the middle of a word it sounds like a soft d	
rr	erre	roll your r's as mentioned above	
S	ese	Like English s	sorry
T	teh	a soft English t, the tongue touches the back of the upper teeth	

V	veh	like Spanish b	boots

Consonants continued

Consonant	How to say the letter	How to pronounce it in a word	As in...
w	dobleveh	like English w	water
x	equis	*Between vowels and at the end of a word, it sounds like the English *ks*. *At the beginning of a word, it sounds like the letter *s*.	*box *sorry
y	igriega	like English y	yellow
z	seta	s	six

Note: If you're not sure how to pronounce a word, one thing you can do is type it in *Google translate* then click on the little speaker icon in the bottom left corner to hear the correct pronunciation.

To check out the rest of *"Learn Spanish In 7 DAYS! - The Ultimate Crash Course To Learning The Basics of The Spanish Language In No Time"*, **go to Amazon and look for it right now!**

Ps: You'll find many more books like these under my name, Dagny Taggart. Don't miss them! Here's a short list:

- Learn **Spanish** In 7 Days!
- Learn **French** In 7 Days!
- Learn **German** In 7 Days!
- Learn **Italian** In 7 Days!
- Learn **Portuguese** In 7 Days!

- Learn **Japanese** In 7 Days!
- Learn **Chinese** In 7 Days!

- Learn **Russian** In 7 Days!

- Learn Any Language FAST!

- How to Drop Everything & Travel Around The World

About the Author

Dagny Taggart is a language enthusiast and polyglot who travels the world, inevitably picking up more and more languages along the way.

Taggart's true passion became learning languages after she realized the incredible connections with people that it fostered. Now she just can't get enough of it. Although it's taken time, she has acquired vast knowledge on the best and fastest ways to learn languages. But the truth is, she is driven simply by her motive to build exceptional links and bonds with others.

She is inspired everyday by the individuals she meets across the globe. For her, there's simply not anything as rewarding as practicing languages with others because she gets to make friends with people from all that come from a variety of cultures. This, in turn, has broadened her mind and thinking more than she would have ever imagined it could.

Of course, as a result of her constant travels, Taggart has become an expert on planning trips and making the most of time spent out of what she calls her "base" town. She jokes that she's practically at the nomad status now, but she's more content to live that way.

She knows how to live on a manageable budget weather she's in Paris or Phnom Penh. She knows how to seek out the adventures and thrills, no doubt, lying in wait at any city she visits. She knows that reflection on each every experience is significant if she wants to grow as a traveler and student of the world's cultures.

Because of this, Taggart chooses to share her understanding of languages and travel so that others, too, can experience the same life-altering benefits she has.

7382255R00049

Printed in Great Britain
by Amazon.co.uk, Ltd.,
Marston Gate.